ROCKS AND SOIL

Steven M. Hoffman

PowerKiDS press

New York

Published in 2011 by The Rosen Publishing Group, Inc.
29 East 21st Street, New York, NY 10010

First Edition

Editor: Amelie von Zumbusch
Book Design: Kate Laczynski
Layout Design: Ashley Burrell

Photo Credits: Cover © www.iStockphoto.com/Jeanne Goodridge; pp. 4, 14 Shutterstock.com; p. 6 Nigel Cattlin/Getty Images; p. 8 iStockphoto/Thinkstock; p. 10 Peter Hendrie/Getty Images; p. 12 Jupiter Images/Photos.com/Thinkstock; p. 16 © www.iStockphoto.com/BasieB; p. 18 Greg Neise/Getty Images; p. 20 © www.iStockphoto.com/James Wright.

Library of Congress Cataloging-in-Publication Data

Hoffman, Steven M. (Steven Michael), 1960–
  Rocks and soil / by Steven M. Hoffman. — 1st ed.
      p. cm. — (Rock it!)
  Includes index.
  ISBN 978-1-4488-2560-8 (library binding) — ISBN 978-1-4488-2706-0 (pbk.) —
  ISBN 978-1-4488-2707-7 (6-pack)
  1. Soil formation—Juvenile literature. 2. Soils—Juvenile literature. 3. Sediments (Geology—Juvenile literature. I. Title.
  S592.2.H64 2011
  631.4—dc22

                                                2010030655

Manufactured in the United States of America

CPSIA Compliance Information: Batch #WW11PK: For Further Information contact Rosen Publishing, New York, New York at 1-800-237-9932

CONTENTS

Volcanoes are not the only places where soil forms on top of bare rock. Here, you can see pockets of soil that formed and plants that started growing on a rocky hillside.

Rock to Soil

The side of the **volcano** was bare. A **lava** flow had cooled into lifeless, black rock. For years, the rock barely changed. Finally, a few strong plants took root in cracks in the rock.

Water, air, and the plants slowly changed the hard rock. Soil began to form. After hundreds of years, a layer of soil covered the black rock. Plants and animals were everywhere.

Rock is a hard solid. It is made of **minerals**. Soil forms on top of rock. In fact, soil has little bits of rock in it. However, soil is softer overall than rock is. Almost all plants need soil to grow.

In this cutaway picture, you can see how roots hold a plant in the soil. You can also see the different bits of matter that make up soil.

A Dirty Mix

Soil has many parts mixed together. Its solid parts include pieces of sand and clay from rocks and matter from living things. Most of the matter from living things comes from plants. Plant roots, leaves, and stems break down and become part of the soil.

Air or water fills small spaces, called **pores**, between the solids. The amount of air or water in soil pores changes. After a heavy rain, pores hold lots of water. When soil dries, the pores hold less water. The water in soil forms a thin coat around the solids. Air fills the rest of the pores. During very dry weather, the pores in soil are filled almost completely with air.

The pounding of waves against rocks along a coast breaks down those rocks a little bit at a time. It is one of many forms of weathering.

Breaking Down Rock

Rock seems never to change, but rock at Earth's surface does break down slowly. Ice, heat, cold, and growing plant roots slowly break it apart. Gravel, sand, and smaller pieces form. Water, air, and **acids** from plants break down rock even more. Some of the rock's matter **dissolves**. Some forms clays and other new minerals.

The changes that break down rock are together called **weathering**. Weathering helps soil form. It makes the small pieces of sand and clay that are in soil. Over time, weathering also changes the mix of matter that makes up soil.

Weathering occurs faster in places that have wet weather. It occurs more slowly where the weather is dry.

Rivers sometimes drop sand in places where they slow down and enter the ocean. This can cause sandbars, such as the ones in this river, to form.

Moving Sediment

Sometimes, the sand and clay that formed by weathering stay in one place and soil forms there. The small grains, called **sediment**, also can be picked up and moved away. The picking up and moving of sediment is called **erosion**. Water and wind cause erosion. Erosion also occurs when sediment falls downhill.

Deep soil forms where lots of sediment piles up. For example, rivers drop sediment along their banks and form deep, rich soil. Rivers also drop sediment where they enter an ocean or lake. These places often have soil that is rich in **nutrients** from the sediment. Valleys have deep soil because sediment from mountains falls to the valley floors.

These mushrooms are fungi. Like bacteria, fungi break down living things after they die. Things that break down plant or animal matter are known as decomposers.

Making Humus

After sediment builds up, plants, animals, and other living things begin to make their homes in it. All of these living things help make soil. Grass and tree roots grow down through the forming soil. Leaves fall onto it. Worms tunnel through it.

When plants or animals in soil die, tiny living things, called **bacteria**, break down their body parts. The bacteria change the roots, leaves, and parts of animals into dark **humus**. Soil that has a lot of humus has a deep black color. It also has large pores and holds water well. This kind of soil is ideal for plant growth.

Soil that has many things living in it is rich. This means that it is good for growing plants.

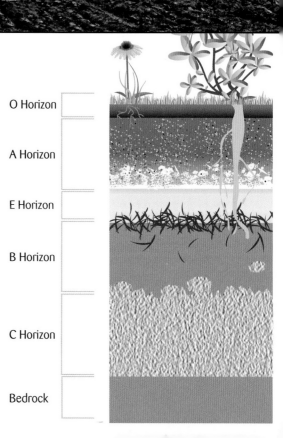

O Horizon

A Horizon

E Horizon

B Horizon

C Horizon

Bedrock

A horizons are often known as topsoils. Most crops grow in these soils. Inset: This drawing shows a soil with many horizons. Bare rock, called bedrock, is at the very bottom.

Layers of Soil

Most soils have several layers, called **horizons**. Horizons are named with letters. Soils commonly have an A horizon on top, a B horizon beneath that, and a C horizon at the bottom. An A horizon is a dark layer with a lot of humus. A B horizon has less humus but has lots of clay that washed down into it. A C horizon's soil has changed little from the sediment from which it formed.

Other horizons also occur. Some soils have O horizons. These are top layers that are made mostly of rotted plant parts. E horizons occur deep within certain forest soils. These layers are white because their dark matter has dissolved, leaving white sand grains.

How acidic soil is makes a difference to the plants growing there, too. Hydrangeas turn blue in acidic soil. Some people add acidic matter to soil to turn these flowers blue.

Soil for Plants

Most plants need soil to grow. Soil holds plant roots in place so that plants can grow tall and strong. Plant roots take in water from soil pores. The water then moves up into plant stems and leaves. Plant roots also need air from soil pores. Plants can die if the soil they are growing in becomes too wet or too dry.

Soil also has nutrients, such as nitrogen, that plants need to grow and stay healthy. The water in soil has nutrients dissolved in it. Plants can take nutrients in only when they are dissolved in water.

People often add plant food to soil. Plant food increases the amount of nutrients dissolved in soil water.

This is Nachusa Grasslands, in Illinois. The parts of the grasslands that were always prairie have a thick A horizon. This layer is less deep on parts of the grasslands that were used as farmland.

Soils of Many Kinds

Different kinds of soils form under different conditions. The sort of sediment soil is formed from and the steepness of the land play parts. The place's **climate** and the plants that grow there do as well.

Grassland soils, forest soils, and desert soils are some of the most common types of soil. Grassland soils have a thick, black A horizon. This is because grasslands produce lots of dead grass roots that become humus. Forest soils have a thinner A horizon. They may have a white E horizon that forms as acids from pine trees dissolve dark matter. Desert soils get little rain, so few plants grow there. These soils have a light color and may have a hard layer below.

The trees on this hillside have been cut down. This makes it easy for the soil to wash away any time that it rains.

Losing Soil

The erosion of soil can be a big problem. The top layer of most soils is better for growing plants than the soil below. If this top layer gets washed or blown away, plants will not grow well.

Farmers often worry about losing soil. Soil erodes easily from plowed fields because no plants hold it in place for part of the year. Many farmers now practice no-till farming. In this method, new seeds are planted in the dead matter from last year's crop. Less soil erosion occurs because fields are never plowed.

Soil erosion is also a problem in places where trees are cut down for their wood. People often cut wood to build homes and furniture. They also burn wood to cook food and provide heat. After trees are cut down, the bare land left behind erodes quickly.

Soil Where You Live

You can learn about soil in many places. You can find natural soil in a park or field near your home. Clearing a small amount of ground will give you a good look at the soil's top layer. Notice the soil's color and openness. Rub some soil between your fingers to find out whether it is sandy or clayey. If there is a small ditch nearby, you might see several layers of soil.

Knowing about soil is important. Someday, it might help you do your job! Farmers, soil scientists, and others need to know a lot about soil. Today, knowing about soil will help you grow healthy plants, whether in a garden or in a small pot.

GLOSSARY

acids (A-sudz) Things that break down matter faster than water does.

bacteria (bak-TIR-ee-uh) Tiny living things that cannot be seen with the eye alone.

climate (KLY-mut) The kind of weather a certain place has.

dissolves (dih-ZOLVZ) Breaks down.

erosion (ih-ROH-zhun) The wearing away of land over time.

horizons (huh-RY-zunz) Layers of soil.

humus (HUH-mis) Dark brown matter formed from the remains of dead plants and animals.

lava (LAH-vuh) Hot, melted rock that comes out of a volcano.

minerals (MIN-rulz) Natural matter that is not an animal, a plant, or another living thing.

nutrients (NOO-tree-ents) Food that a living thing needs to live and grow.

pores (PORZ) Spaces between the solid parts of soil that are filled with air or water.

sediment (SEH-deh-ment) Gravel, sand, or mud carried by wind or water.

volcano (vol-KAY-noh) An opening in the surface of Earth that sometimes shoots up lava.

weathering (WEH-thur-ing) The breaking up of rock by water, wind, and chemical forces.

INDEX

WEB SITES

Due to the changing nature of Internet links, PowerKids Press has developed an online list of Web sites related to the subject of this book. This site is updated regularly. Please use this link to access the list:
www.powerkidslinks.com/rockit/soil/